The Girls' Book of Friendship

HOW TO BE THE BEST FRIEND EVER

Written by Gemma Reece
Illustrated by Katy Jackson
Edited by Sally Pilkington
Designed by Zoe Quayle

The Girls' Book of Friendship

HOW TO BE THE BEST FRIEND EVER

Buster Books

First published in Great Britain in 2010 by Buster Books,
an imprint of Michael O'Mara Books Limited,
9 Lion Yard, Tremadoc Road, London SW4 7NQ

www.mombooks.com/busterbooks

Text and illustrations copyright © Buster Books 2010
Cover design by Angie Allison (from an original design by www.blacksheep-uk.com)

A CIP catalogue record for this book is available from
the British Library.

ISBN: 978-1-906082-88-8

2 4 6 8 10 9 7 5 3 1

Printed and bound in England by Clays Ltd, St Ives plc

Papers used by Michael O'Mara Books are natural, recyclable products
made from wood grown in sustainable forests. The manufacturing processes
conform to the environmental regulations of the country of origin.

NOTE TO READERS

CONTENTS

HOW TO MAKE A FRIENDSHIP LOCKET

A friendship locket is a pendant, worn around the neck, that opens to reveal pictures of your best friends. Wearing one means that you can keep your friends close to you, even when you are apart.

You will need:

• scissors • a pencil
• 2 small photos of your friends • a sheet of pretty gift wrap
• a small metal hinge 2.5 cm x 2 cm (from a DIY shop)
• 50 cm ribbon • PVA glue

1. Take your length of ribbon and thread it through one of the holes at the top of the hinge.

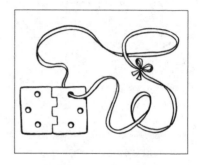

2. Turn your pretty piece of paper over, so that it is patterned-side down. Place the hinge open on top, and draw around it. Cut this out so you are left with a rectangle. Cut this rectangle in half, widthways, so that you have two small rectangles.

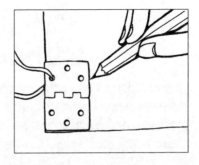

3. Apply a thin layer of glue to each side of your hinge and stick each rectangle on to it, positioning it by sliding it around while the glue is still wet. Be careful not to position them too closely so that the locket opens easily. Leave this to dry.

4. When your hinge is dry, take one of your photos and position the closed hinge over the part you want to appear in your locket. Draw around the hinge and then cut the shape out. Repeat this with your other photo.

5. Place your hinge so that it is patterned-side down and carefully apply a thin layer of glue to the inside faces. Take one of your photos very carefully by the edges and stick it to the hinge so that the head points towards the ribbon. Repeat for the other photo and then leave your locket open to dry.

6. Once the glue is dry, close the locket and wear it around your neck.

HOW TO HELP A FRIEND IN NEED

One of the most important things in a friendship is helping each other out when one of you is going through a tough time. Follow these dos and don'ts to make sure that you are being a good friend when your best mate is feeling blue.

DO 'be there' for your friend. This means finding the time to be with her, even if you are busy. If she is very sad, you might want to try and rearrange your plans so that you can spend extra time with her.

DO show your friend you care. Call her when you are not together, or send her a little card, to let her know that she is not alone and that you are thinking of her.

DO offer advice. If your friend comes to you with a problem, try to help her find a solution. If her problem seems very serious, encourage her to turn to an adult you both trust to help her work out what to do.

DON'T be upset with your friend if she doesn't take your advice and decides to do her own thing. It's her life after all.

DON'T go on and on about a time when something similar happened to you. This is your friend's problem, so give her the space to talk it out.

DO stock up on cookies and tissues. Let your friend have a good cry on your shoulder, and share some cookies with her (see page 34). Soon she'll be well on the way to feeling fine again.

HOW TO BUILD UP TRUST WITH YOUR FRIENDS

How much do you trust your friends? Find out with these frantic but fun trust games, which aren't about winning or losing – you all need to work together or it's game over!

WE ALL STAND TOGETHER

This game shows how much easier life is when you work together and lean on each other for support.

Stand back to back with your friend, with your shoulders touching hers, then lock your arms together with hers at the elbows.

Now, very slowly, try to sit down on the floor without unlocking your arms. This is much more difficult than it sounds.

Once you have managed to sit down, do not unlink your arms. Instead, try to stand up again. This is even more difficult and can leave you in some very funny positions.

True-friend tip. Make this game even more fun by asking another friend to join you as you try sitting down and standing up again, locked together as three. Keep on adding people until all of your friends are in the circle!

11

FALLING FOR YOU

This game is the ultimate test of friendship and proves that you can always rely on your friend to catch you when you fall.

Stand with your back to your friend, about half a metre away from them. She must then reach her arms out towards you and be ready to catch you. All you need to do is fall back on to her arms. You really need to trust your partner for this.

As you fall, try to keep your body as straight as you can, and don't take a step backwards.

It sounds simple, but you'll soon see it takes a while to pluck up the guts to fall on your friend!

True-friend tip. Make sure you read the instructions carefully and give each other your full attention to avoid any accidents.

THE MINEFIELD OF FRIENDSHIP

This game shows you how listening to your friends can help you to overcome obstacles and avoid disasters. Is your friendship strong enough to survive the 'minefield'?

Ask your friend to leave the room for a few minutes.

While she is out of the room, set up the 'minefield' or obstacle course. Keep it simple – for example, move a chair into the middle of the room for her to avoid, and place piles of cushions on the floor to weave around.

When you are happy with your minefield, cover your friend's eyes with a blindfold and lead her back into the room. You now need to call out instructions so that she is able to walk around the minefield avoiding all of the obstacles. All she can use to guide her are your instructions – no peeking allowed. If your friend touches an obstacle or knocks anything over, switch places and let her set up the minefield while you wait outside.

COPYCATS

In any group of good pals, each friend gets her chance to take the lead. You will need at least four friends to play.

Form a circle with your friends and ask one of them to leave the room for a few minutes. She will be the 'Guesser'. The rest of you have to decide who is going to be the 'Leader', making everyone left a 'Copycat'.

Invite the Guesser back into the room and allow her to rejoin the circle. The Leader and the Copycats must now start swinging their arms backwards and forwards.

While you are all swinging your arms, the Leader must also make other small movements, such as sticking out her tongue or tapping her foot. The Copycats must copy these movements as soon as they see them without making it at all obvious who it is they are copying. The Guesser must watch very closely and try to work out who the Leader is.

When the Guesser has managed to identify the Leader, it is the Leader's turn to become the Guesser so that the game can start again.

True-friend tip. To make the game super-challenging, the Leader should discuss which movements they are going to use with the Copycats before the Guesser comes back into the room, that way the Copycats will know what to look out for and be able to copy her mega-fast.

HOW TO MAKE A FRIENDSHIP SURVIVAL KIT

This pretty pouch of trinkets is simple to make and is the ideal gift for someone close to your heart. It will remind them of what their friendship means to you.

You will need:

- a large clean handkerchief • a ball of cotton wool
- a piece of gold thread or gift ribbon
- a small candle • a button • a sticky plaster
- a pebble • a small roll of sticky tape
- a piece of writing paper (A5 is best) • a pen

1. Lay the handkerchief out in front of you and place all of the items into the middle of it, leaving out the gold thread, the writing paper and the pen.

2. Take your piece of paper and, in your best handwriting, write out the friendship survival kit's user guide on the next page.

THIS FRIENDSHIP SURVIVAL KIT CONTAINS:

- A golden thread, because friendship is the golden thread that ties our lives together

- Some cotton wool, to cushion any rocky roads ahead

- A candle because you are a shining light

- A plaster for healing hurt feelings

- A handkerchief for drying your tears

- A pebble because you are my rock

- Some sticky tape because good friends stick together

- A button because if you can't say anything nice – button your lip!

3. Fold your survival kit's user guide in half and then in half again until it is as small as you can make it, and then pop it in the centre of your handkerchief with the other items.

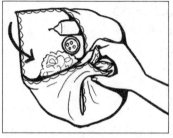

4. Gather the corners of your handkerchief together to form a pouch.

5. Tie your gold thread or gift ribbon around the top in a pretty bow to keep your items inside.

6. Give your survival kit to a good friend to let her know you will be her BFF (Best Friend Forever).

HOW TO SHOW THE WORLD YOU'RE FRIENDS

Okay, so you know who your friends are, now it is time to let others in on the secret. Follow these top tips to show the world who your fave people are.

GET A 'BEST-FRIEND' HANDSHAKE

When you meet up with your friends, performing your own personal handshake is the perfect way to prove you are best buds. A best-friend handshake needs to be loud and bold so that other people can see and hear it. You can either make up your own, or use the one below.

1. Stand opposite your friend and gently bump your right fist against hers.

2. Do the same with the left fist.

3. Clap your right hands together and slowly slide them backwards and apart.

4. End with a big back-slapping hug.

GET THE LOOK OF FRIENDSHIP

Wearing exactly the same clothes as your friend can look a bit over-the-top and is a definite fashion no-no. Co-ordinating your look, however, is totally cool. For example, if one of you wears black jeans and a white top, the other should wear white jeans and a black top. This can look seriously stylish and will get you loads of attention.

BE BUDDIES, BRIGHT AND BEAUTIFUL

Choose a colour that you both like and try to wear an item in that colour every day. At school, keep it simple – for example, add a purple hair band, or wear a lilac vest under your shirt to show that you are friends without alerting the uniform police. You can go wild with your chosen shade at the weekend.

MAKE A NAME FOR YOURSELF

Really close friends never call each other by their real names, but use nicknames instead. To come up with nicknames for yourself and your friends, make up silly words based on your real names, such as 'Lyndependent' for Lynn, or 'Maxibaby' for Maxine. Alternatively, use nicknames that are to do with your personalities – for example, if one of your friends is always laughing, they could be called 'The Giggler'. Don't be afraid to mix things up a bit – a friend who is very tall could be called 'Shortie', or a friend with very dark hair could be called 'Blondie'.

True-friend tip. Make sure you agree your names together. Calling someone a name that she doesn't like or agree to is not cool or friendly. It could hurt her feelings and even get you into some serious trouble.

HOW TO MAKE A FRIENDSHIP COAT OF ARMS

A 'coat of arms' is a shield made up of pictures that represent the person who owns the shield. In medieval times, they were used by knights to identify who they were on the battlefield. Make your own as a symbol of your friendship group.

You will need:

- an A3 sheet of card • a ruler • scissors • a pencil
- felt-tip pens • old magazines • a glue stick
- a photograph of you and your friends
- a picture of where you all live

1. Using your pencil, draw this shield shape on to your sheet of card as large as you can and then cut it out.

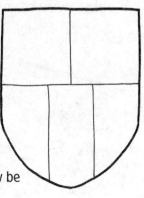

2. Use a ruler to draw a line dividing the shield in half, as shown. Divide the top half of your shield in half again.

3. Divide the bottom portion of your shield into three as shown. Your shield should now be divided into five sections.

4. Take the photo of you and your friends together, and glue it in the top left-hand section of your shield.

5. Together, go through all of your old magazines and look for a picture of the thing you all love best. For instance, if you can't get enough of eating delicious ice cream, try and find a really cool picture of a sundae, or if you all really love dolphins, find a picture and cut it out. If you can't find a picture, don't worry, simply draw it on a fresh sheet of paper and cut it out. Stick this in the top right-hand section of your shield.

6. In the bottom left-hand section, put in a picture of where you all live. You could find a postcard of your town or village and cut that out to stick in, or take a photograph of a popular landmark.

7. In the bottom right-hand section, put in a picture to represent someone who you all admire and look up to. If they are famous, look for a picture in your magazines and snip it out, or if it is someone you know, take a photograph.

8. Now you should think of a motto for your friendship group. A motto is a phrase that sums up the things you all think are most important. For example, 'Laugh loud. Laugh lots.'

True-friend tip. Your coat of arms is very precious as it is a symbol of your friendship. Take it in turns to look after it and make sure you keep it safe.

WHAT KIND OF FRIEND ARE YOU?

Ask yourself the following questions and note the answers **A**, **B** or **C** down on a piece of paper. The results will reveal how you fit into your friendship group.

1. Your friend asks your opinion on a new top that she was given as a present, as she thinks it might be a bit ugly. You think that the colours really clash. Do you ...

  A. ... say that you think it might be a little over-the-top and that she could try to exchange it – but add that she looks good in anything?

  B. ... laugh and tell her you wouldn't be seen dead in it and neither should she?

  C. ... suggest that she wears it out and starts a new fashion? If she won't, you will!

2. You see some friends having a water fight in the park, but you are supposed to be going home to do your chores. Do you …

A. … wave, and arrange to meet them later after you have been home and completed your tasks?

B. … run to the shops and buy some balloons to fill with water, then run back to the group and attack?

C. … continue on your way? You'll have some cold lemonade to cool off while you're doing your chores.

3. At school, a friend gives you a note telling you she's been feeling down in the dumps. Do you …

A. … arrange to meet her at lunchtime with all your other mates so you can give her a hug and find out her problem?

B. … give her a hug, pull a weird face and mess your hair up to make her laugh?

C. … write a note back and ask what's wrong?

4. Your birthday is coming up. Do you …

A. … wait until the day, then take slices of your birthday cake into school to share with everyone?

B. … make sure everyone knows what day it is and invite your whole class to your party.

C. … ask your parents to take you and your best friend on a trip to the local water slides?

5. Two of your friends have had an argument. Do you …

   A. … talk to them separately, tell them how important it is to you that you are all friends, and try to encourage them to see each other's point of view?

   B. … immediately ditch them in favour of some new friends who seem to be more fun?

   C. … leave them to it? It is better not to get involved. They will get over it in time, they always do!

6. Your friend confides in you that she has a huge crush on a boy in your class at school. Do you …

   A. … share your secret crush with her, and spend hours together coming up with ways that you can accidentally 'bump into' the boys on the way home from school?

   B. … immediately start talking to the boy and his mates so you can become better friends with him and get him on good terms with your friend?

   C. … do nothing? You'll keep her secret but it's her business. You're not that bothered about boys anyway.

7. The most important thing in a friendship is …

   A. … helping each other through the bad times and caring for each other.

   B. … giggling together, making up silly games and generally having fun. The more friends the better!

   C. … spending quality time with close friends and giving each other space to do your own thing.

MOSTLY **A**S – CARER-SHARER

You are the one who everyone turns to in a crisis. You are calm and kind, and love to look after people and help them to feel better. You don't have just one best friend, but are happiest in a group of several close friends. Beware, you can be a little over-sensitive at times.

MOSTLY **B**S – PARTY PRINCESS

Your friendship group is always changing and getting bigger. You love to be the centre of attention and love causing a commotion by being loud and silly. You see your friends as companions for fun, and try not to take anything too seriously. You do tend to be a little bit impatient sometimes, so try to chill out once in a while.

MOSTLY **C**S – MISS INDEPENDENT

You tend to have one best friend who is important to you, and if she's not around, you don't mind spending time on your own. You don't rely on others for things to do and generally don't mind what other people think of you. Sometimes you can be a little too unsociable, so make sure you venture out more.

HOW TO MAKE A FOUR-WAY FRIENDS' PIZZA

Takeaway pizzas can be quite expensive, and agreeing what toppings to have on them is a nightmare. Avoid the rows and save the pennies by getting three of your friends together to help make this delicious treat.

You will need:

- 225 g self-raising flour • ½ teaspoon salt
- 55 g butter, cut into small pieces
- 50 ml water and 50 ml milk combined
- 5 tablespoons tomato pasta sauce
- a variety of yummy toppings such as grated cheese, chopped ham, chopped mushrooms, sliced pepper, prawns, olives, pineapple chunks, flaked tuna, sweetcorn, etc …

1. Ask an adult to pre-heat the oven to Gas Mark 7/220°C.

2. Pour the flour into a large mixing bowl and then add the salt and the butter.

3. Rub the butter into the mix by squashing it with flour between your fingers and then sprinkling it back into the bowl. Lift your fingers high above the flour. Do this until there are no lumps of butter and the mixture looks like breadcrumbs.

4. Pour in half the milk and water and stir with a table knife. When all the liquid has been absorbed, add more liquid until the mixture starts to stick together.

5. Get your hands into the bowl to squash your mixture into a soft dough. If your dough feels very sticky, add a little more flour.

6. Sprinkle some more flour on to your work surface and roll the dough into a large circle about 1 cm thick, using a rolling pin. Then transfer it on to a baking sheet.

7. Spoon the pasta sauce on to your base, and spread it out using the back of a spoon.

8. Now, get creative with your quarters, putting on any toppings that you like and finishing with a layer of cheese before asking an adult to pop it into the oven for 15 minutes.

9. Ask an adult to remove it from the oven. Leave the pizza to cool for about 10 minutes and then enjoy.

THE GOLDEN RULES
OF FRIENDSHIP

Follow the golden rules of friendship to make sure you are friends forever.

THE RULES

DO laugh things off. You can solve a lot of problems if you don't take everything too seriously. Friends that can laugh together, stay together.

DON'T be a gossip. Never say anything about your friend behind her back that you wouldn't say to her face – unless you are worried about her and are asking for some advice.

DO keep secrets secret. Your private conversations must always stay between the two of you unless you think she might be in danger.

DON'T be a drama queen. Make sure you allow each other an equal amount of time to talk about your problems and what's going on in your lives.

DON'T steal what's hers – whether sweets, ideas, clothes or friends. If your friend doesn't want to share, respect her wishes.

DON'T pick on her faults – unless you are prepared to admit to your own. It is important to be honest with your friend, but only if you are prepared to be honest with yourself first.

DO keep changing. It is unrealistic to think that you and your friend will stay exactly the same forever and want to do the same things. If you always stick to the same routine when you see each other, you'll get bored.

DON'T say, 'I told you so' – even if she does something you don't approve of. Do your best to put yourself in her shoes and support her even when she doesn't take your advice.

DON'T be a taker-backer. If you've given something to a friend to keep, never ask for it back, even if you stop being friends – it is the same as breaking a promise.

DO learn to forgive. It is easy to be angry with your friend when she hurts your feelings, and you may want to hurt her back. Make sure you listen to your friend's apology and forgive her if you think she means it. (See page 105.)

HOW TO MAKE A TEAM T-SHIRT

These fresh and funky Ts are super-fun to make. Wear them whenever you and your best friends go out together, and people will be able to spot your friendship team from a mile off!

You will need:

- rough paper • a clean white T-shirt each • cardboard
- a pencil • fabric pens • fabric paints

1. Get together with your friends and come up with a team name. Jot some ideas down on a piece of paper. Your team name can be anything you like. If you all love playing sports, you could be, the 'Sporty Sistas'. Or if you all love things that are girly and sparkly, you could call yourselves the 'Glam Stars'. It doesn't matter what your name is, but you all have to agree on it.

2. Now decide on an 'emblem'– a picture to represent your team. Make sure it is something that you can all draw and that fits with your team name. For instance, if you called your team the 'Glam Stars' you could choose a picture of a crown over a star, like this.

LET'S GET SHIRTY

3. Place the cardboard inside the T-shirt, so that the fabric is stretched flat. This will make it easier for you to draw your design on to it, and will stop the paint going through to the other side.

4. Use a pencil to draw your emblem on to the top right-hand corner of the front of your shirt, about 12 cm down from the shoulder. Write your team name in block capitals underneath. Make sure it's big and noticeable.

5. With the cardboard still in place, go over your team name and the outline of your emblem with fabric pen and then leave it to dry.

6. Use a paintbrush to fill in your emblem with fabric paint. Put your shirt to one side to dry.

7. Once it's dry, turn your T-shirt over and design the back. Use a pencil to write your name or nickname (see page 18) across the shoulders of your shirt in bold letters, then draw your emblem (larger than you did on the front) underneath. Write your team name below.

8. Go over your team name and the outline of your emblem with fabric pen and then leave it to dry.

9. Paint in your emblem as you did before and then leave it to dry.

10. To fix your design so that your shirt can be worn and washed again and again, follow the instructions on the pack of your fabric paints and pen. Most fabric paints are fixed by placing an old piece of cotton fabric on to your design and ironing over it with a hot iron. Ask an adult to do this for you.

True-friend tip. Why not decorate your design with sequins? Simply glue sequins, or buttons and bows on to your shirt using fabric glue.

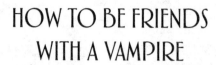

HOW TO BE FRIENDS WITH A VAMPIRE

Vampires might have a bad reputation but, let's face it, they're also pretty cool. They can fly, wear cool dark-coloured clothes, and they get to stay up as late as they want every night. Follow these top tips to bag yourself a brand new blood-sucking buddy.

Know where they hang out. Check your local graveyards or any castles in the area. The beach or the playground is a complete no-no. All that sunshine is a killer for their pale skin.

Avoid the local pizza parlour. Vampires call it 'garlic central' and vampires hate garlic. If you walk around smelling of garlic, you can guarantee they won't come anywhere near you.

Dress the part. Dark colours are best. Jewellery is fine, but steer clear of anything cross-shaped if you don't want to upset your new vampire buddy. Vampires are terrified of crucifixes.

Don't try to get your new pal to change her image. You will only hurt her vampire feelings. Vampires 'live' for a very long time, so she may have been dressing like that for centuries.

Protect her identity. If you think your friend is a vampire, it is best to keep it to yourself. Some people get a bit freaked out by the idea of being friends with the undead.

Don't bother trying to take her photograph. You won't be able to. True vampires can't be captured either digitally or on film, and most can't even be seen in mirrors.

Avoid going to sleepovers at her house. Sleepovers with vampires aren't much fun, unless you enjoy spending all day trying to get to sleep in a dusty coffin. Invite her to stay over at yours instead. Having a friend who won't go to sleep when you want to make a midnight feast can be very handy.

Don't get too close. Hugging is fine, but if she tries to give you a kiss on the cheek, just say, 'No, fang you!'

HOW TO MAKE
FRIENDSHIP COOKIES

People say that the way to a girl's heart is through her stomach – so if you want to make yourself really popular among your friends, why not make a delicious batch of friendship cookies? Take a box of these cookies when you go to see your friends, and they will soon be begging you to tell them the recipe!

You will need:
- 250 g porridge oats
- 125 g chocolate chips
- 125 g soft brown sugar • 2 eggs
- 125 g softened butter

1. Ask an adult to preheat the oven to Gas Mark 5/200°C.

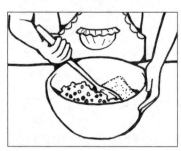

2. Tip the oats, chocolate chips and sugar into a large bowl and mix together well.

3. Crack the eggs into a small jug by tapping each one against the rim of the jug until the shell cracks, and then gently pull the two halves apart.

4. Beat the eggs together with a fork until all of the yellow of the egg and the clear bit are combined.

5. Stir the beaten egg slowly into the oat mixture, and then gradually add the butter, stirring constantly until you have a rough dough.

6. Use your hands to make small conker-sized balls out of the dough, and squash these on to a baking sheet.

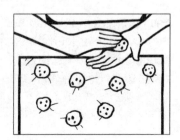

7. Ask an adult to put the baking tray into the oven and bake for 8 minutes.

8. Ask an adult to remove the cookies using oven gloves. Put the tray to one side to cool.

9. When the cookies have cooled, slide them off the tray using a palette knife and put them into an airtight box ready to take to your friend's house.

True-friend tip. You don't really need an excuse to make cookies, but these little circles of goodness are perfect for spreading cheer amongst your friends. Scientists have proven that oats and chocolate contain special chemicals that can actually cheer you up when you are feeling blue. Why not give a batch to a friend who is feeling down? These yummy treats are sure to put a smile on her face.

WHY EVERYBODY NEEDS GOOD FRIENDS

You don't have to be the most popular girl at school, or have an address book as fat as the telephone directory, but everyone should have a few special friends to share happy times and sad times with. Here's why:

FRIENDSHIP IS ...

… talking about your biggest fears and finding out that they are the same.

… laughing together at a joke that nobody else finds funny until tears stream down your face and your sides hurt.

… discussing your deepest, darkest secrets and trusting that they will never be revealed to anyone else.

… knowing that your friend is unhappy even before she tells you something is wrong.

… having someone who will let you know that your skirt is tucked into your knickers before anyone else sees you.

… sharing the homework as well as the birthday cake.

… making plans for brilliant things to do together at weekends and in the school holidays.

… trusting that she won't laugh at you if you fall flat on your face, even if everyone else does.

… writing long letters to your friend when you are on holiday telling her all of your news, and giving them to her when you get back.

… having someone to share a large bucket of popcorn with at the cinema.

… not being able to wait until the next day to speak and picking up the phone as soon as you get home from school.

… having someone that knows you so well it is a bit scary – she even knows what you are going to say or do before you do.

… knowing that she will always be there for you, even if you mess up in a big way.

HOW TO MAKE A FRIENDSHIP FLOWER

Gather a bunch of your best buddies together to make a floral feel-good boost that will last for ages.

You will need:

• scissors • a saucer • a pencil
• sheets of thin card in different colours • a glue stick • a pen

1. Give each friend a sheet of card. Take it in turns to place the saucer on to the card and draw around it using a pencil.

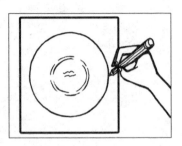

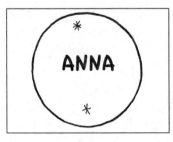

2. Cut out your circles. Each girl should then write her name across the middle of her circle of card in bold letters. These will be the centres of your friendship flowers.

3. Cut petals from the rest of the card. It is easiest to cut out one petal first and then use it as a template to draw around. Your petals can be any shape you like, but make sure there is enough room to write on them.

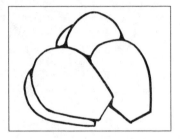

4. Once there are enough petals for each girl to have at least five each, the floral fun can really begin. Choose one girl to go first and say her name out loud. Each girl then has to write down something that she thinks is fantastic about that person on to a petal. It could be, 'She can pull the funniest faces,' or, 'She is fantastic at football'. When you are finished, hand the petals to the person in question.

5. Go around the group, doing the same thing for each friend in the group. Keep going until each girl has at least five petals in front of them.

6. Apply a thin layer to the bottom of each petal using a glue stick and stick it to the back of the paper circle so that the writing on it can be seen from the front, as shown below.

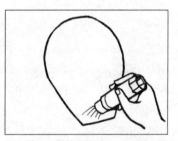

7. You can either stick your flower on the wall at home, or keep it somewhere safe and look at it whenever you need reminding what a special person you are.

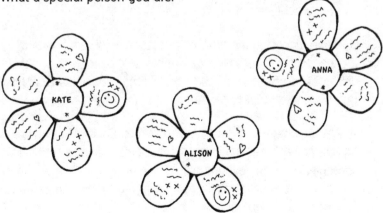

HOW TO USE 'THE POWER OF PALS'

Mates are great for having a laugh and chatting with, but did you know you can also use the power of your friendship to help you achieve your wildest dreams?

GOAL-GETTING GALS

Whether you are trying to save your pocket money to buy something special or learning a difficult dance routine, some goals seem like they are out of reach. Here is how pal power can help:

1. Gather a group of gal-pals with similar goals to you and choose a day and a time that you will meet up each week for your 'check-in' session. Monday lunchtime is a good choice, as you will start the week with a positive attitude.

2. Agree on your target – for example, growing your nails to the end of your fingertips – and agree a date that you are aiming to achieve it by.

3. Make a chart in the back of a notebook with each of your friends' names across the top and the date of each check-in down the left-hand side. Add lines to make spaces to fill in how you are doing at each check-in.

4. At your check-in, take it in turns to talk about how you are doing. Use this time to encourage each other and offer tips. For example, if you have found a special nail varnish that stops you biting your nails, this is your chance to share the secret. Record each of your friends' progress in your chart.

5. When you have reached the end of your chart, celebrate together, even if everyone hasn't quite reached their goal.

TWO HEADS ARE BETTER THAN ONE

Pal power can also help to make even the most boring assignments much easier and fun. Each of you has different strengths – here's how to use those strengths to make your friendship an unstoppable force.

DO work together. When you have a project from school and you don't know where to start, arrange a 'Brain Power Day'. On this day, meet up with friends in your local library or at someone's house, and see what fun facts you can find out.

DO help each other. If you are really good at maths but numbers freak your friend out, help her out with her sums. In exchange, she can help you with something you struggle with and that she finds a breeze. This way, your homework will fly by, you'll have fun at the same time.

DON'T copy each other's work. You could end up helping each other into a lot of trouble with your teacher.

41

HOW TO SORT OUT SQUABBLES

There will be squabbles and arguments among even the closest group of friends. This time two of your best pals aren't speaking to each other. This is not fun, especially if you're made to feel that you have to take sides. Sort out your arguments quickly and fairly by setting up your very own 'Court of Friendship'.

TWO SIDES TO EVERY STORY

1. Invite the friends who are rowing to meet you and the rest of your friends at a time when you are all free. Lunch break is perfect, or sometime after school or at the weekend.

2. When you are all gathered together, ask another friend to be the chairperson, or take this role yourself. The rest will be the jury.

3. Once all the roles have been given out, give each squabbling friend three minutes to explain her side of the story. The chairperson must make sure that they stay calm and give all the information needed, such as what they believe happened, and why they behaved the way they did.

DECISION TIME

4. The rowing friends must then leave the room while the chairperson and jury decide what should be done. Try to consider both sides and to remember that the most important outcome is that everybody stays friends. Your job is to come up with a way of making this happen. For example, if Friend A has borrowed Friend B's top and torn it, you may conclude that, as it was only an accident. Friend A does not have to replace it, but Friend B can borrow an item of clothing of her choice from Friend A.

THE VERDICT

When you have decided on what to do, invite the rowing friends back in and let them know your decision. Ask them to shake hands or hug – and smile at each other.

True-friend tip. You may find that once they have heard each other's explanation of what happened, the squabbling friends are able to come up with a solution themselves. Whatever happens, make sure you aren't too harsh in your sentencing or the argument will continue and could even get worse.

HOW TO MAKE A SUPER-FAST FRIENDSHIP BRACELET

These cool and funky bracelets are quick to make and great fun to wear. Get together and make gifts that you and your mates will love.

You will need:

• scissors • a bulldog clip • a sheet of thick card
• embroidery thread in five colours • a ruler

1. Measure and cut a length of embroidery thread 45 cm long. Use this piece as a guide to cut a piece of each of the other colours to the same length.

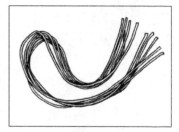

2. Hold all five pieces of thread together, and fold them in half. Tie them together in a knot about 5 cm from the loose ends.

3. Clip the bulldog clip on to your sheet of card with the knot underneath and the rest of the thread hanging down.

4. Separate out each colour and hook three colours around the

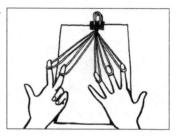

index, middle, and ring fingers on your right hand, then the two remaining colours around the index and middle fingers on your left hand.

5. Move the thread from the index finger on your right hand to the empty ring finger on your left hand, as shown. Keep the threads nice and taut so they don't get tangled.

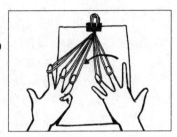

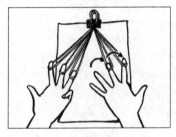

6. On your right hand, shift the threads up two places so that they are now on the index and middle fingers.

7. Now move the thread from the index finger on your left hand to the ring finger of your right hand. Keep pulling the threads out tightly.

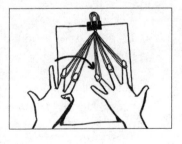

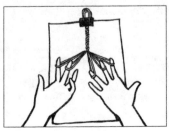

8. Repeat steps **5** to **7** and keep going until you are 5 cm away from the ends of your threads. Your bracelet should now be long enough to tie around your friend's wrist.

9. To finish, remove the bracelet from the clip and loop it around your friend's wrist. Secure it in place with a double knot.

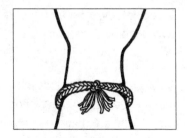

10. Once you and your friend have tied the bracelets around each other's wrists, try to keep them on for as long as possible, as a sign of your friendship.

IMAGINARY-FRIEND FUN

You've got best friends, pen friends and maybe even friends who are boys. However, did you know that you could have a great friendship with someone who doesn't exist outside your own head? Here are some reasons why imaginary friends are fab.

- You don't have to limit yourself to normal human friends. Why not make friends with a celebrity or even an animal?

- Your imaginary friend will never steal your style – you can dress her up any way you like and she won't argue with you.

- She'll be with you at all times. Every night can be a sleepover, and those terrifying thunderstorms won't be that scary anymore.

True-friend tip. Instead of keeping a diary, try writing your thoughts down as letters to your imaginary friend. You might find that you share a lot more when you direct your thoughts to a friendly ear.

HOW TO MAKE A FRIENDSHIP BOX

Give this special gift to a friend to promise her that you will always be there for her.

You will need:

- an empty matchbox • scissors • a pencil • a photo of you and your friend together • a glue stick • coloured gift wrap • a small piece of coloured writing paper • confetti • ribbon

1. Slide out the inner tray of your matchbox and place it on top of your photo. Draw around it using a pencil, then cut the photo out and glue it inside the bottom of the tray.

2. With your gift wrap patterned-side down in front of you, place the matchbox lengthways in the bottom left-hand corner and draw around it. Slide the matchbox up the paper so that the bottom edge sits on the top line and draw

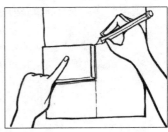

around it again. Repeat this once more so that you have one long rectangle made up of three matchbox shapes.

3. Cut out the long rectangle shape and then cover the plain side with a thin layer of glue.

4. Place the outer sleeve of your matchbox on the bottom edge of the long rectangle and wrap the paper around it neatly. Leave it to dry.

5. Meanwhile, take your small sheet of writing paper and copy out this poem in your best handwriting. Or you can make up your own, it is up to you.

THE FRIENDSHIP POEM

Here inside this friendship box
A most important message lies.
I placed it here for you to find
It's only for your eyes.

Treasure the note inside this box
And keep its message inside your heart.
It's a sign we'll be friends for life,
Nothing can ever make us part.

So if you're down and feeling blue
This box was sent to say,
'Good times or bad, I'm here for you
I promise that, today.'

6. Fill the rest of the box with confetti to spill out when your friend looks to see what is inside.

7. Slide the box inside the outer sleeve and then tie it up with ribbon in the same way you would tie up a parcel. Finish with a pretty bow.

True-friend tip. Why not give a friendship box to a friend to cheer her up if she is sad, or to say you are sorry if you have had a falling out? However, remember, if you are given one, you must look after it and treasure it forever as a sign of your eternal friendship.

HOW TO HAVE THE ULTIMATE PYJAMA PARTY

Sometimes there aren't enough hours in the day to hang out with your friends, and that is why a great gal-pal from long ago invented the pyjama party. Here are some handy hints for making yours a night to remember.

THE TOP TEN PYJAMA-PARTY ESSENTIALS

DO have a dress code. Cute pyjamas and the snuggliest socks are the height of sleepover chic.

DO play by your parents' rules (as much as possible). Keeping the noise down is the only sure-fire way of keeping them out of your hair for the evening.

DO make a pyjama-party play list. Each guest should bring their top three CDs to play. Play the louder songs at the beginning of the night and save the quiet, mushy ones to play on low volume when you are supposed to be 'sleeping'.

DO make sure you are well stocked with chocolate. Ask each girl to bring a bar of her fave choc treat and then share and share alike.

DO pick out some cool DVDs to watch together. Only scary, funny or weepy ones will do.

DO try out new hairstyles on each other. Get each girl to bring along her brush and all of her cool clips, bands or curlers and then go wild. The joy of a sleepover is that no one will see your hairstyle if it looks crazy.

DON'T forget to set your alarm clock. Midnight is the best hour for confiding secrets and devouring feasts, so make sure you don't miss it.

DON'T forget magazines. Get each girl to bring as many current and old issues of her fave mags as she can carry so that you can all flick through and decide on who your favourite superstar is.

DON'T let anyone leave the room until they have revealed all about their secret crush.

DON'T forget the ice cream! Everyone should bring a tub of their favourite flavour, then tip it into a giant bowl to create an ice-cream dream, or just eat it straight from the tub with a teaspoon. Teaspoons just make it taste better.

WHEN IS A FRIEND NOT A TRUE FRIEND?

Some people can seem like they are your friends, but they're nowhere to be seen when you need a shoulder to cry on. Here's how to tell a true friend from a fake friend.

A TRUE FRIEND WOULD NEVER ...

... persuade you to do something you don't want to do – whether it is something embarrassing to entertain them, or something that you think is wrong.

What to do. Try to stand up to them and explain that a real friend wouldn't want you to do anything that would make you feel uncomfortable. If they don't listen, steer clear and find a true friend who will like you for who you are.

A TRUE FRIEND WOULD NEVER ...

... turn other friends against you. If one friend has decided she doesn't want to be your friend any more, she might try to stop other people hanging around with you, too.

What to do. Try speaking to your friends one-to-one to explain what is happening. If they don't want to know, ditch them – you don't want to be friends with people like that anyway. If it is happening to you, it is sure to be happening to someone else, too. Look out for girls going through the same thing as you and make friends with them.

A TRUE FRIEND WOULD NEVER ...

... put you down in public. If your friend makes nasty comments or jokes about you in front of other people it can make you feel small and very silly. It might seem like she is just trying to be funny, but if she is hurting your feelings then she is not acting like a true friend.

What to do. Wait until you are alone with your friend and explain to her how she is making you feel. She may not have realized that she was hurting your feelings and might promise never to do it again. If she still doesn't stop, try to spend less time with her, and spend more time with other, truer, friends.

A TRUE FRIEND WOULD NEVER ...

... borrow your things without asking or take money from you. Everyone likes to help their friends out by sharing and maybe even treating them to some sweets if they don't have any pocket money left, but they should never make you feel bad by hassling you.

What to do. Let other friends know what is happening, or confide in an adult that you trust.

A TRUE FRIEND WOULD NEVER ...

... reveal your secrets. Friendship is all about trusting each other, and it can feel terrible when you feel like the trust between you has been broken.

What to do. Ask your friend why she revealed your secret and remind her that you only told her on the understanding she would not tell anyone else. If she is sorry, forgive her, but be careful about telling her any secrets in future until you are sure that she is able to keep them.

True-friend tip. Girls can sometimes treat their closest friends badly to make others like them more. They do this because they feel unhappy or insecure, but it isn't fair if it makes you feel bad. If you have tried to speak to your friend about how she is upsetting you, and she doesn't stop, she doesn't deserve your friendship.

Friends are there to make life better and more fun, so the time they stop being a friend is when you come away from seeing them feeling bad.

YOU KNOW YOU SPEND TOO MUCH TIME TOGETHER WHEN ...

Being best friends is brilliant, but did you know that there is such a thing as spending too much time together? No? Answer true or false to the statements below to find out if you and your friend are in danger of becoming a terrible two-headed monster.

TRUE OR FALSE?

• Her parents automatically set you a place at the table for dinner, even when you're not there.

• You cry every time your friend goes on holiday. It feels like nothing this tragic has ever happened to you before.

- You turn up at parties wearing identical outfits, completely unplanned.

- When someone asks a question, you answer the same thing at the same time.

- Your mum and dad have her school picture next to yours on the mantelpiece.

- You know your friend is going to call even before your phone rings.

- Your handwriting is exactly the same as hers.

- Your other friends merge your names into one – for example, if your names are Jo and Lucy, they call you 'Juicy', or Katy and Jemma and they call you 'Kemma'.

- New people you meet can't believe you're not sisters.

THE RESULTS

If your answer was 'true' to four or more of the statements above, you and your friend are spending too much time together and are in danger of merging into one monstrous bi-headed being. You need to take action before it's too late.

WHAT TO DO

It is great to be best friends, but it is important to have your own identity, too. Good friends let each other be themselves and value each other's differences rather than trying to be exactly the same all of the time. Try taking up different hobbies – this will not only give you more to talk about when you see each other, but it will also help you to make some new mates.

HOW TO MAKE A FRIENDSHIP FORTUNE FINDER

Find out what the future has in store for you and your friends with this funky fortune finder.

You will need:

- 1 sheet of A4 paper • scissors • a pen
- felt-tip pens or colouring pencils

1. With the longest side of the paper at the bottom, fold the top right-hand corner of the paper, so that the right-hand edge lies along the bottom edge. This will leave you with a rectangle of paper on the left-hand side. Trim this off using your scissors. You should now have a folded triangle of paper.

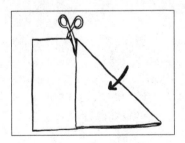

True-friend tip. To make your fortune finder super-neat, smooth down each fold you make firmly with your fingertips.

2. With the longest side of the triangle at the bottom, fold the triangle in half so that the right-hand corner completely covers the left-hand corner. Smooth down the fold.

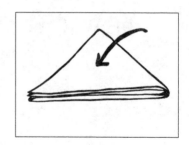

3. Repeat step **2** to make an even smaller triangle.

4. Open up your triangle to reveal a square of paper with lots of creases running through a central point.

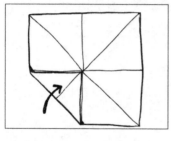

5. Using the creases as a guide, fold this square into a smaller one by folding each corner of the square into the centre point.

6. Turn your paper over and repeat step **5** to make an even smaller square.

7. Turn your square over. You should be able to see four square flaps of paper. Colour each of these flaps a different colour using your felt-tip pens or colouring pencils.

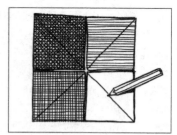

8. Turn your square over again, and write a single number from 1 to 8 in each of the triangles you can see.

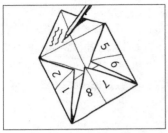

9. Unfold the top triangle and write one friendship fortune on each side of the crease. Your fortunes can be whatever you like but keep them mysterious and fun. Here are some you could try:

- Wear something pink and you will make a new friend.

- On Tuesday, someone you love will misunderstand you.

- Beware of frogs and toads – they may not be all they seem.

Repeat this for each of the triangular flaps until you have written eight friendship fortunes, then fold all the flaps back to the centre to make a square.

10. Fold your square in half lengthways to make a rectangle with two of your coloured flaps showing on each side.

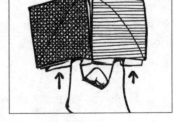

11. Pull each of the four flaps out using your thumbs and index fingers, and push the tips up and into the middle.

FUN WITH FORTUNES

To work your finished fortune finder, hold it with your thumbs and index fingers together so that all four of the coloured flaps are showing. Ask your friend to pick a colour. To find her fortune, open and close the fortune finder once for each letter in the word. For instance, if your friend picks 'BLUE', open and close the fortune finder four times and finish with the finder open. Ask you friend to pick a number from the inner flaps that she can see. Open and close the fortune finder this number of times, finishing in the open position. Ask her to choose another number. Lift the flap with this number on it to reveal your friend's fortune.

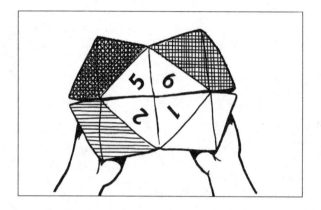

True-friend tip. Fortune finders are so easy to make, why not make lots for different areas of your life? You could make one about love with fortunes such as, 'A gorgeous boy will offer to lend you his bike,' or one about school, for example, – 'Make sure to finish all of your homework for teachers with dark hair.'

FIVE REASONS WHY PETS MAKE GREAT FRIENDS

Reason one. Walking the dog is brilliant exercise and a great way to get out into the park for some fresh air.

Reason two. A cat is the perfect TV companion – it'll keep your lap warm but never talk through your favourite show.

Reason three. You can't share your sweets with pets, it will make them sick. What a shame, more sweets just for you.

Reason four. Your pet will never disagree with your opinion or laugh at you when you do something silly, but they will always be on hand for a cuddle when you're feeling blue.

Reason five. You can whisper all your secrets to your pet and be sure they'll never tell (unless you have a talking parrot, of course).

REAL FRIENDS OR FAKE FRIENDS?

Real friends are friends you can trust will always be there for you. Fake friends will be around while everything is fun but will be nowhere to be seen when the going gets tough. Here's how to tell a real friend from a fake one.

A REAL FRIEND SAYS ...

- 'Of course you can borrow my favourite top.'

- 'What's up? You can talk to me about it if you want.'

- 'I promise you can trust me.'

- 'I would love it if you'd come to my birthday party!'

- 'We'll meet you in the park, by the swings, at 3pm.'

A FAKE FRIEND SAYS ...

- 'What will you give me in return?'

- 'Oh, just cheer up, will you?'

- 'Ooh, tell me – I love secrets, they're so exciting!'

- 'You can only come to my birthday party if you bring your new karaoke machine/ cool older sister ...'

- 'Erm ... yeah ... we'll probably meet you in the park at some point later ...'

HOW TO SEAL YOUR FRIENDSHIP

A 'ritual' is a ceremony that is made up of special words and actions, performed in a specific order. Performing a friendship ritual will seal your friendship and bring good luck to you and your friends. This one is for two or more people to perform together.

You will need:

• a clean tablecloth or blanket • some squash in a jug or flask
• a cup for each friend, plus one extra
• a personal item from each friend, such as a favourite
photograph or a home-made gift

SETTING THE SCENE

Lay the tablecloth on the ground. Somewhere outdoors is best, for example in the corner of your back garden or under a tree in the park.

Ask each friend to lay their chosen item in the centre of the cloth and then to take a seat beside their items on the cloth.

LET THE SIPPING BEGIN

Pour the drink into one of the cups and then ask everyone to take it in turns to drink a little from the cup, but to make sure that they leave enough for the next person. Share any liquid left in the cup between the rest of the cups and give one to each friend. You should then say:

'With the sharing of this drink, we agree
to share our lives together for evermore.'

PUT YOUR HEART INTO IT

Now it is time to pass your personal items around the group. The item could be a favourite photograph or even a friendship box (see page 47) or a friendship bracelet (see page 44). Ask each girl to pick up her personal item from the cloth and pass it to the girl on her left. The girl giving the item should make the following promise:

'This *insert name of item here* is a symbol of who I am.
By giving it to you I promise that you will have
a piece of my heart forever.'

After these words have been spoken, the girl receiving the item should say:

'I accept this *insert name of item here* as a symbol of who
you are, and promise to treasure it and
your friendship forever.'

THE SACRED RING

When all the items have been exchanged, ask your friends to link hands and close their eyes to sing the sacred song of friendship below.

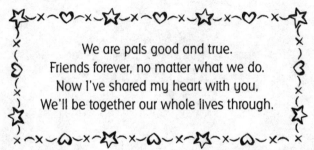

We are pals good and true.
Friends forever, no matter what we do.
Now I've shared my heart with you,
We'll be together our whole lives through.

True-friend tip. Ask each friend to try to memorize the words before the ceremony, unless, that is, they are able to read with their eyes closed …

FRIENDS FOREVER

Congratulations! You are now friends forever. Each time you have an argument or a falling out, remember this ritual and how you felt when you made these promises to one another. It will make it much easier to forgive each other and go on being friends.

HOW TO MAKE A PERSONALIZED BIRTHDAY CARD

Much cooler than any card you can buy from a shop, transform an old one into the perfect personalized card. Give your friend a card she will REALLY like for her next birthday.

You will need:

- an old birthday card • scissors • a sharp pencil
- modelling clay • a glue stick • sticky tape
- a photo of your friend • old newspapers or magazines
- one sheet of plain paper

1. Make a hole in the parts of the card you want to cut out by pushing a sharp pencil through the card into a lump of modelling clay underneath.

2. Remove the pencil and modelling clay, and carefully insert the point of your scissors into the hole you have just made. Cut out the areas of the card that will become your windows.

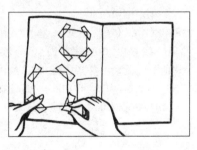

3. Choose a nice photo of your friend and some photos of her fave celeb or pets cut from old magazines. Check they are the right size to show through your windows, by placing your card over them. Cut them out, leaving an extra bit around the edge for sticking.

4. Position your pictures behind the windows in the front of your card and then stick them down on the inside using pieces of sticky tape.

5. Lay your card out flat on to a sheet of plain paper and draw around it using your pencil. Lift it off and cut the shape out so that you have a piece of paper the same size as your card.

6. Apply a thin layer of glue on to the inside of your card and on to the piece of paper using a glue stick. Stick the paper on to the inside of our card to cover up any old messages and the sticky tape.

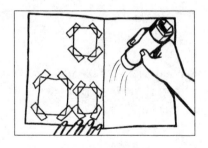

7. When the glue has dried, write in your very own birthday greeting and give it to your friend.

True-friend tips. Don't stop at birthdays. Use this method to make cards for your friends for Christmas or other holidays. Why not put yourself into some really funny scenes to cheer your friend up when she is down? Don't use an old birthday card with an age on the front, unless it is the age that your friend is about to be!

HOW TO 'GO FISH' FOR FRIENDS

Here's a fun card game that you can make at home, which you not only can play with your friends, but which features them as part of the game, too.

You will need:

- 3 A4 sheets of thin card
- a glue stick • 4 photographs (1 of you and 3 of your friends)
- a pen • scissors • lots of old magazines or a computer and printer • felt-tip pens

1. Take a sheet of card and divide it into eight equal rectangles by folding it in half once lengthways, and then twice widthways. Unfold and repeat with the other two sheets.

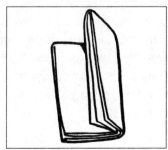

2. On one of your sheets of card write your name at the top of one of the rectangles. Do the same with the names of your three best friends at the top of three other rectangles.

3. Use a glue stick to fix your picture, and the pictures of each of your friends underneath their names.

4. Underneath the picture, write the following headings: 'Fave colour', 'Fave animal', 'Fave food', 'Fave celeb', 'Fave hobby', and then write in what each of these favourites are for your friends.

5. Go through all of your old magazines and look for the pictures for each of your friends' favourite things, that match all of the headings listed in step **4** (except favourite colour) and cut them out. If you can't find them all, then why not have a look on the internet? Once you have found as many as possible, ask a parent or whoever owns the computer if it would be okay for you to print them out.

6. Once you have as many pictures as you can find, you can start filling in the rest of your rectangles. Glue each picture into the centre of a rectangle and write the name of the person whose favourite it is across the top of the card and label it underneath. For example: 'Anna' across the top, and 'Fave hobby: Karate' underneath.

7. For any pictures that you can't find, simply draw a picture of your friend's favourite thing and then colour it in.

8. For the favourite colour cards, write each name on the top of a card and then use felt-tip pens in each person's chosen colour to draw a squiggle in the centre of the card. Label the colour underneath.

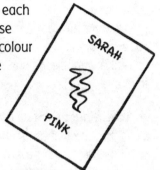

9. When you have filled in all of the rectangles on each of your sheets of card, cut them out so that you have 24 separate cards.

True-friend tip. To make your cards last for lots of games, cover both sides of each of the A4 pieces of card with sticky-back plastic before cutting them out.

TO PLAY THE GAME

You will need between two and six players.

1. Shuffle your cards, and deal them out one at a time, face down, to each of the players until there are none left.

2. Each player should look at the cards she has, but hide them from the other players. The aim of the game is to collect a full set for each friend.

3. The player on the left of the dealer starts. She must ask the next player round the circle for a particular card that she needs. For example, if she already has Claire's photo card and Claire's favourite colour card, she might ask, 'Do you have Claire's favourite food?'

4. If the player she has asked has that card, she must hand it over, and the first player, to the left of the dealer, has another go. If she does not have this card, she must say, 'Go fish,' and then take her turn as in step **3**.

5. The player who collects the most full sets, wins.

True-friend tip. Listen very carefully to what your friends ask for when it is their turn. This will give you clues as to what they have in their hands and what you could ask them for when it is your turn.

HOW TO DRAW A SILHOUETTE OF YOUR FRIEND

Drawing silhouettes is an easy way to make a really cool piece of artwork in an exact likeness of your friend. Take it in turns to pose for a silhouette, using the instructions below.

You will need:

- 3 sheets of A3 white paper • 2 sheets of A3 black paper
- a pencil • a lamp • scissors • sticky tack • a glue stick

1. Stick a sheet of white paper to the wall using sticky tack (check with a parent first to see if it is okay to use sticky tack on the wall you wish to use).

2. Position your lamp so that it will shine directly on to the paper.

3. If it is daytime, close the curtains and try to block as much natural light out of the room as possible. If you are doing this in the evening, turn off all of the lights other than your lamp.

4. Ask your friend to stand or sit sideways on to your sheet of paper, in front of the lamp.

5. Move the lamp around until you can see your friend's shadow very clearly on the piece of paper.

6. Use a pencil to draw all the way around the outline of your friend's shadow very carefully.

7. Take the sheet of paper down and cut the shape of your friend's silhouette out to make a template.

8. Place your template on a piece of black paper and draw around it. Cut this out.

9. Glue the black silhouette on to a fresh sheet of white paper using a glue stick.

10. Now ask your friend to draw your silhouette following steps **1** to **7**.

11. Stick the white silhouette of you directly on to a sheet of black paper – this will mean your picture will contrast with your friend's picture.

12. Mount your works of art in pretty frames or simply stick them up on your wall in pride of place using sticky tack.

True-friend tip. Why stop at black and white? Experiment with different, cool colour combinations for a really funky work of art. A hot pink silhouette on a blue background would look great, or even one cut from patterned gift wrap.

HOW TO HOLD A FRIENDSHIP AWARD CEREMONY

An award ceremony is a cool way of showing your mates how much you care about them. It can take place at someone's party or a sleepover, or you can even just get everyone together one day after school.

PLANNING

First you have to think up the categories. Here are some ideas:

Funniest friend

Most-stylish friend

Best listener

Cleverest friend

Most-loyal friend

Best friend at giving advice

Most-sporty friend

Fairest friend

Oldest friend

Most-patient friend

You and another friend can make up the judging panel.
To make it fair, only one prize can be awarded to each friend,
and everyone should get a prize. Write your choices down
on a piece of paper and keep them secret and safe until
he ceremony.

PRIZES

For your awards, you need something extra-special that your
friends can all wear with pride. These badges are perfect, and
they're very easy to make.

You will need:
- a sheet of coloured card (A4 is best) • a piece of thin,
white paper • a pencil • a glitter pen • scissors
• safety pins • sticky tape

1. Place the piece of thin, white paper on top of this star shape and carefully trace around it using your pencil. Cut it out. This is your template.

2. Place the paper star template in the bottom left-hand corner of your coloured card. Draw around it using your pencil.

3. Move your template to the right and draw around it again. Repeat this until your whole sheet of card is filled with star shapes. Cut them all out. These are your badges.

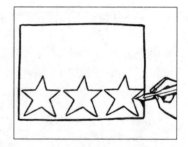

4. On each badge, write the name of the winner and the award with a glitter pen. For example: 'Molly, Funniest Friend'.

5. When the writing is dry, attach a safety pin carefully to the back of each star with the sticky tape. Make sure you stick down the fixed side of the pin rather than the pointy end.

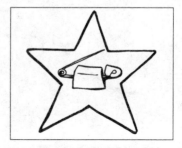

True-friend tip. To make your award badges super-special, decorate them with blobs of glitter glue and sequins.

AND THE WINNER IS ...

During the ceremony, present the correct badge to each winner. You should give your reasons for your choices – for example, 'Nina was chosen as the Most-Stylish Friend because she can always find the right outfit for every occasion, and even manages to make her school uniform look cool.'

THE FRIENDSHIP SURGERY

Dr Bigheart specializes in taking your poorly friendships and making them healthy. Here are her answers to some of the most common friendship dilemmas.

LETTER ONE

Dear Dr Bigheart,

There's a girl in my class who everyone ignores. I feel sorry for her and would like to make friends with her, but I'm worried if I do that, my own friends will laugh at me and start to ignore me, too.

DR BIGHEART SAYS ...

'Don't worry about things that haven't even happened yet.
If you want to start including this girl, do it, but take it one step
at a time. Making an effort to smile and say, 'hello' to her in
the mornings is a good place to start. Then try including her in
conversations when she is nearby. If you do this casually, your
friends will not feel threatened or worry that you are going off
with this other girl. They'll probably leave you to it. Good on
you for being so considerate of this girl's feelings – your mates
should copy your example!'

LETTER TWO

Dear Dr Bigheart,

My friends seem to get a lot more pocket
money than me and their parents always seem
to be buying them new clothes. I feel really
uncool compared to them, it's not fair.

DR BIGHEART SAYS ...

'Being cool is not about money and clothes. Your mates must
think you're pretty cool to like you in the first place, regardless
of how many pounds are in your purse. If you want a new
look, why not go through your wardrobe and try out new
combinations. Remember being cool is based on who you are,

not what you buy or what you wear. You have your own value and strengths, whether it's making people laugh or coming up with new ideas. Stay strong!'

LETTER THREE

Dear Dr Bigheart,

One of my best friends has been acting very strangely lately. She keeps going off and sitting on her own at lunchtime and seems so moody. She used to be really chatty but now she's always quiet. Do you think I have done something wrong?

DR BIGHEART SAYS ...

'It sounds to me like your friend has got a big problem on her mind, and it isn't necessarily something you have done. Perhaps she has got some problems at home that she feels too upset to talk about. Try to get her alone and let her know that you are worried about her. Ask her if there is anything you can do to help. If she refuses to talk, it may be worth talking to a teacher or adult that you know and trust, and telling them about how she has changed. They may be able to find out what is wrong. Good luck, and well done for being such a caring friend!'

HOW TO MAKE A BASE CAMP

Make your own base camp so you and your friends will be able to hang out there without being interrupted by pesky adults. Here's how to set it up.

FIND YOUR BASE

You'll need somewhere big enough for you to all sit down with room for your supplies, too. How about ... an attic? A space in your garage? Or even a corner of your bedroom? Any spot you can call your own.

CUSTOMIZE AND COSY IT UP

To make your camp look gorgeous, you'll need to get creative. Here are some ideas:

• Put a big pinboard up on the wall so that you can cover it in posters and change the pictures easily to show who and what you're into that week.

• Buy, beg or borrow some fairy lights to make your base camp instant girlie heaven.

• Keep a big box marked 'supplies', packed with your secret stash of goodies ... sweets, cartons of drink, magazines and games.

• And, of course, you'll each need somewhere to sit down, so why not make your own personalized cushion covers?

HOW TO MAKE BASE-CAMP CUSHIONS

You will need:

• an old cushion • fabric • scissors • pins • a needle
• thread in a similar colour to your fabric • fabric paints
• old newspaper • a paintbrush • fabric glue
• buttons and sequins

1. Cut out a piece of fabric that is twice the size of your cushion, with an extra 5 cm added to its length and width.

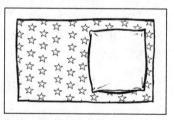

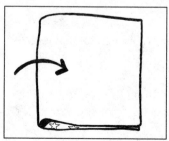

2. Fold the fabric in half. If it is patterned, make sure the patterned side is on the inside.

3. Pin the edges of your fabric together using sewing pins, leaving one side of your square open.

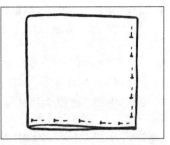

4. Thread your needle with 1½ m of thread and tie a double knot in the end. Push the needle through the bottom left-hand corner of the cushion cover and pull through on the otherside up to the knot.

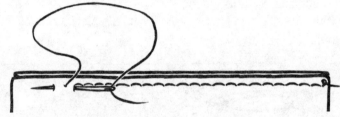

5. You are going to sew along this outer edge in a straight line, no more than 1½ cm in from the edge. Pull the needle back through the fabric about 1½ cm ahead of your original point and again gently pull the thread through. Now, go back and push the needle back through, in the same place you did at first. Keep pulling the thread through quite tightly. Then push the needle through, roughly 1 cm ahead of the last point.

6. Continue sewing until you are about 1½ cm from the next edge. Turn the corner and sew along as you did in step **5** with the other pinned side of the cushion. When you reach the top right-hand corner secure your stitches by sewing over the same spot ten times. Cut off any excess thread.

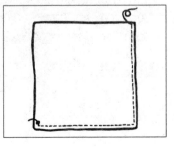

7. Turn the cushion cover inside out and place a piece of newspaper inside to protect the other side of the fabric.

8. Decorate your cushion with fabric paints. You could paint on your team emblem (see page 30) or whatever you like. Make sure you mark your cushion with your initials so everyone knows who it belongs to. When you have finished, glue on your sequins and your buttons and then leave it to dry.

9. Insert your cushion and sew up the final side by folding the loose edges inside 1½ cm and then pinning both sides together. Sew this side up over the pins just as you did before.

True-friend tip. Once your base camp is complete, why not ask your parents if you can use it as the venue for an awesome pyjama party (see page 50)?

HOW TO MAKE UP AFTER AN ARGUMENT

So, it's happened – you had a disagreement which turned into a row, and before you know it, the two of you aren't speaking any more. It can happen very easily! But there's no need to stop being friends, you just need to learn the art of making up.

MAKE HER LAUGH

Making her laugh is a foolproof option. If she's a good friend, you'll have a decent idea of what is guaranteed to make her chuckle. Get it right and she won't have any choice but to let that frown melt into a bout of giggles. Here are some ideas:

- Catch her eye and pull your silliest face.

- Ring her up and sing a silly song down the phone.

- Jog her memory by asking if she remembers the hilarious time when you ...

WRITE HER A 'SORRY' CARD

A 'sorry' card is the option to choose if you feel that you were in the wrong in the argument. Choose or make a card with 'sorry' on the front, and inside write your apology straight from the heart. Explain your reasons for doing what you did, and say that you hope she will forgive you and move on.

BRIBE HER

Nothing wins a friend back better than buying her back! Say you'll take her to the cinema with your pocket money, buy her a magazine, or even lend her your brand new top. She'll be like putty in your hands.

HOW TO MAKE SURE IT NEVER HAPPENS AGAIN

Once you have made up, you need to make sure this never happens again. To do this, you need to perform a sacred make-up ritual. Sit opposite your friend and link the little fingers of both your hands together. With your little fingers linked together move your arms up and down as you repeat the sacred rhyme together:

Make friends. Make friends.
Never, ever break friends.
If you do I'll throw you down the loo,
and that will be the end of you.

HOW TO MAKE A FRIENDSHIP MEMORY CAPSULE

You might not believe it now, but when you are grey and wrinkly you may find it hard to remember all the fun you had with your friends when you were younger. Make a memory capsule filled with mementos to remind yourself of the good times you are having together right now.

You will need:

- a biscuit or chocolate tin • acrylic paints in various colours
- a permanent marker • some pens • masking tape
- a sheet of writing paper and an envelope for each of you
- a collection of mementos and messages
from you and your friends

1. Wash out your tin with soapy water to get rid of any bits of old biscuit or chocolate. Rinse it and leave it to dry.

2. Paint the outside of the tin and the lid in a pale colour, such as pale blue or yellow, and then leave it to dry. You need to use acrylic paints for this as these will stick better to the outside of the tin.

3. Decorate the inside base of the tin by painting on a pretty pattern. You could paint on a heart or flowers or even use your friendship emblem (see page 30). When you are finished, put the tin to one side to dry.

4. On the lid of the tin, use your permanent marker to write in bold letters the date when you want to open your tin – for example, 'DO NOT OPEN UNTIL AUGUST 2050'. Leave it to dry.

5. Meanwhile, choose the items that you are going to put into the capsule. Think of the memories you want to preserve for the future. Good things to put into your friendship memory capsule include:

- photographs of all of you together
- pictures of your favourite singers and film stars
- programmes and mementos from things you have done together, including plays you have acted in/been to together, old cinema tickets from your favourite films, or newspaper cuttings about sporting events you have been to.

6. Give a piece of writing paper, an envelope and a pen to each of your friends and ask them to write a letter to be read out to the group when the memory capsule is opened. The letters can be about anything you like – for example, a story about a fun time you have shared together, or what you like best about each of your friends. You could even write about what you hope each of your friends will be doing when you open the box.

7. When you have all finished your letters, ask your friends to put them into the envelopes and seal them.

8. Gather together all of the letters and put them inside your friendship memory capsule with the collection of mementos.

9. Put the lid on the capsule and seal it shut by covering over the join between the tin and the lid with lots of layers of masking tape.

10. Ask each friend to write their initials on the tape using a permanent marker. This way you will all know that no one has snuck a peak inside the capsule before you come to open it.

11. Hide the memory capsule somewhere it will not be found for many years. This could be in the attic, at the back of your wardrobe, or under your bed. You could even ask your parents' permission to dig a hole and bury it in the garden.

True-friend tip. Don't forget to take the capsule with you if you move house. The new owners of your house might not take kindly to a bunch of ladies banging on their door in 40 years' time, demanding to look for a friendship capsule in their attic.

HOW TO MAKE FRIENDS WITH YOURSELF

Did you know that you have already met the person who knows you best in the world? Someone who will always be there for you, will always take the time to listen to your problems and cheer you up. Follow these top tips to make friends with and look after the best pal you will ever have – YOU.

- Don't take things too seriously. If you feel grumpy, slap a big smile on your face. You'll find it hard to be grouchy while you're smiling.

- Write yourself a list of five good things you've done at the end of each week. It could be anything from learning how to do the front crawl, to getting a merit at school.

- Be a friend to your body. Don't spend all of your spare time in front of the TV or computer – get outside and do some exercise.

- Give yourself a pat on the back every time you achieve something. After all, that's what you'd expect a friend to do.

- Spend some quality time with yourself. Learn how to enjoy yourself even if you're not hanging out with friends. You can use the time to read, get creative, or just chill out – you deserve it!

HOW TO MAKE FRIENDS WITH A CELEBRITY

The life of a star can seem so glamorous – parties, award ceremonies, and international fame, but celebrities are just normal people underneath! Here's how to become friends with a celeb.

DON'T get too star-struck. When you spot a star, try to stay calm. This can be tricky when your stomach is doing somersaults, but if you treat the celeb like you would a normal person, they are more likely to want to become your friend.

DO make them laugh. Instead of immediately asking about the latest film or song they worked on, why not try asking them a silly, random question to make them laugh? Try, 'Do you dunk your biscuits in your tea or just eat them alongside?' or, 'Which do you prefer, sharks or dolphins?' Your idol will be so pleased to have the chance to talk about something other than their career, that they will warm to you straightaway.

DO be loyal. Just like your other friends, celebrities are only going to be your friend if you are genuine. If they suspect you are only interested in them because of the fun parties they can get you into, they will move on before you can say, 'VIP area, please'.

DO join their fan club. Not only will you get special access to their official websites, but you will receive information on where your celebrity will be appearing next before anybody else does. That means you will be first in the queue for an autograph, and therefore have a better chance to get chatting to them.

DO write letters or send emails to your favourite star. This will not only let them know that you care, but some celebrities have even been known to write back.

DON'T be too upset if they don't write back, or just send a standard letter. Celebrities are very busy people and may not have time to answer every letter.

DO get friendly with up-and-coming stars. Okay, so let's be honest – ending up best pals with a Hollywood A-lister is a little unlikely, but maybe you know a really good actor who you think might hit the big time. Get on their Christmas card list now, before it's too late!

HOW TO GIVE A MAD-CAP MAKEOVER

Getting together and giving each other a mad cap makeover is the best fun and a brilliant way to play around with the way you look. Use any or all of these crazy makeover ideas to create some seriously 'stylish' looks.

HAIR-RAISING IDEAS

Sit your friend down in a chair with her back to you and stand behind her. Ask her to brush through her hair first to get rid of any tangles and then get stylin'. Here are some ideas:

For long locks – bigger is bolder. Start with dry hair and 'backcomb' sections of her hair to create a wild, shaggy look.

To backcomb, take a section of hair about 2–3 cm wide and hold it above her head with your left hand. Take a comb in your right hand, and hold it about 3 cm up from the roots. Gently comb the hair, in short strokes, towards her scalp until it begins to fluff up. Take care not to pull. Do this on a few sections on the top of her head and then smooth the rest of her hair over the top.

For short styles – the spike is right. Start with wet hair and use hair gel or wax to sculpt your friend's hair into crazy spikes and shapes, and then leave it to dry. Finish with a generous spritz of glitter spray.

True-friend tip. Use hair mascara in bright, contrasting colours to make eye-catching stripes all over your friend's hair.

Warning. Unless you want to lose a friend and/or risk a serious telling off, do not under any circumstances pick up a pair of scissors and start cutting her hair. Hairdressing should be left to the grown-ups.

CLASHING CLOTHES

Ask each of your friends to bring some of their clothes over, and create some cool new outfits by mixing and matching each others' styles. Here are a few ideas:

All bright now. Try combining all the brightest items of clothing to make one crazy, clashing, colourful outfit.

Potty for patterns. Checks, stripes, polka dots – throw them all together to create a weird and wacky look that will make your eyes go funny if you look at it for too long.

More, more, more. Don't forget the accessories – the more bling the better. You could go for lots of bangles or bracelets, large rings and chunky pendants.

MIND-BLOWING MAKE-UP

Forget 'the natural look' and get ready to make a statement. Ask your mum very nicely if she has any old make-up she doesn't mind you using, or simply save up all the free samples that come on the front of magazines.

Eye-catching eyes. Using a bright eyeshadow, gently smudge colour over your friend's eyelids, right up to her eyebrows. This will give an extreme, rock-chick look.

Look-at-me lips. Use a shocking pink or red lipstick, and make a feature of your friend's lips, or only dab the lipstick on to the very centre of her top and bottom lips, like a Japanese 'geisha girl'.

Check-me-out cheeks. Whether you choose a golden bronze shade or a pretty pink blush, brush it on to your friend's face – either in sweeps starting from her cheek and moving up into her hairline, or make little rosy circles on each of her cheeks for a doll-like look.

THE BIG REVEAL

Finally, show her how she looks in the mirror, and get ready for her to get her revenge on you – once she has stopped giggling. Take lots of pictures of each other looking your silliest, but remember to get yourselves looking back to normal again before you leave the house.

HOW TO CREATE YOUR OWN 'FRIENDSPEAK'

Let's face it, there are times when you need to keep your conversations private – whether it's to stop your little brother eavesdropping, or to discuss your latest crush. There is only one sure-fire way to make sure your chats don't become the subject of a school scandal or family dining-table discussions, and that's to switch to 'friendspeak'.

INGENIOUS INITIALS

Talk to your friends and come up with a set of codes to use when you need to discuss private things in public places. A quick and simple way of doing this is to take the initials of who you are talking about, and use two different words starting with those letters.

So 'Mark Hill' would become 'Monsieur Horse' and 'Robert Johnston' would become 'Rhubarb Jelly'.

This is an easy way to keep identities a closely guarded secret.

CRYPTIC CLUES

Describe people and places without actually saying the names. The swings in the park could be 'the dangly chain seats'… the sweet shop could be 'the source of all things sweet and lovely'… and school could be 'the house of major dullness.' Your parents could be 'the old squad' or 'the noseys'. Now invent some of your own!

THE 'FRIENDSPEAK' DICTIONARY

Use the words below to confuse nearby adults and anyone not in your gang so that you can talk freely without being understood. Come up with a few 'friendspeak' phrases of your own and jot them down below.

WORD	MEANING	EXAMPLE
Moreish	Good-looking	'Alex looks so moreish today.'
Offside	Amazing	'That film was totally offside.'
Celery	Boring	'Assembly was so celery.'
Cash in!	Yes, definitely!	'Chips for lunch? Cash in!'
Log off	No way	'Wear my pink top? Log off.'
Simmer	Calm down	'It's not that bad. Simmer.'
....	....	....
....	....	....
....	....	....
....	....	....
....	....	....
....	....	....

THE DOS AND DON'TS OF SAFE FRIENDSHIPS

Whether you are out and about with old friends or online with new ones, it's important to be aware of your personal safety so that you can have fun without putting yourself into any danger. Here are a few things you can do to make sure your friendships are safe.

DON'T give out any personal details when you are chatting online. Personal details include: your full name, your school, the details of any of your friends and any part of your address other than your town. If anyone pesters you for this or wants to meet you, log off right away and let an adult you trust know about it.

DO stand up for yourself. Don't be encouraged to do things that you wouldn't normally do just because everyone else is doing it.

DO tell your parents exactly where you are going when you go out. This isn't just so they can have control over your life – it's because they need to know where you are if you don't get back on time.

DON'T confuse harmless mischief and real trouble. Playing silly games and pranks is exciting, but getting involved in activities which could cause danger or upset to you or anyone else is serious stuff.

DO trust your 'gut instinct' – this is the feeling you get when you know what is happening is not right. If you think you should leave a situation or tell an adult, then do so right away.

TEN REASONS WHY BOYS MAKE GOOD FRIENDS, TOO

You might think they're noisy and smelly, and go out of your way to avoid them, but boys can actually make great friends. No, really! Here's why:

Reason one. Got a problem? Talk to a boy – their view on the situation might make you see things differently.

Reason two. Boys are great for adventures, making dens, building tree houses and inventing obstacle courses.

Reason three. If they are upset with you, boys will just come right out and tell you what is wrong instead of getting into a sulk or ignoring you.

Reason four. Boys can always be persuaded into doing dares for your amusement – and can come up with some brilliant ones for you to do, too. See page 107 to get you started.

Reason five. Boys are not afraid of getting scuffed knees when you're playing a game – great for when you want to climb trees or learn to break dance.

Reason six. If you ask nicely, he might lend you his old skateboard and teach you how to use it. Totally cool!

Reason seven. It's always nice to have someone around who makes you feel more sophisticated and funny.

Reason eight. Boys have the best collections of computer games, and often know all of the sneakiest cheats and shortcuts to secret levels. Brilliant!

Reason nine. They can give you some top tips for wowing your team on the football pitch.

Reason ten. They can give you the insider info on that boy you have a crush on.

True-friend tip. Believe it or not, boys have feelings too. Make sure you apply the same golden rules of friendship to them as you would to your gal-pals (see page 27).

HOW TO TELL IF ONE OF YOUR FRIENDS IS A WEREWOLF

Day to day, werewolves can appear to be completely normal human beings, only turning into their wolf form when there is a full moon. Could one of your friends be leading a double life as a mythical monster? Here are the key signs to look out for.

SIGNS OF THE WOLF

• Her room is covered in what looks like animal hair, but her only pet is a goldfish.

• She will make up weird excuses to stay at home and avoid seeing you whenever there is a full moon, but then seems very tired the next day for a girl who claims to have had an early night.

- She hates going to the park. Dog whistles play havoc with her ears, even though you can't hear them.

- Her hair and nails grow really, really quickly, and she always seem to be due for a trim.

- The day after the full moon, your local paper reports that a strange, hairy being was seen prowling through a local farmyard, and prints a blurry picture of the beast. You can't be sure, but you could almost swear the monster was wearing … your friend's favourite pink trainers!

- When she sings along to her favourite pop song, it sounds like howling.

WHAT TO DO

DON'T panic. There are no reports of a real werewolf ever being discovered, let alone having attacked a human being.

DO stock up on your friend's favourite biccies. Werewolves love sweet things even more than you do.

DON'T tell anyone of your suspicions. They may start to tease your friend or even think that you are completely bonkers.

DO save any jars you can't open until she comes round. Werewolves are really strong and are always happy to help.

True-friend tip. Werewolves are the most loyal friends you can ever make, but watch out for the face-licking. Yuck!

HOW TO HAVE THE WINNING SMILE

Good mates are great to have a giggle with, but sometimes it can be fun when there is no giggling allowed. This game is a brilliant way to start a party or to liven up a quiet afternoon.

Stand with your friends in a circle facing each other. Choose one friend to be the 'Smiler'. The rest of you need to keep your faces as straight as possible – strictly no smiling allowed.

The Smiler must then start to smile – the biggest smile she possibly can. Once she is smiling, she must then reach her hand to her face and wipe it across her smile as if she is 'taking off' her smile. She must then reveal her smile-free face and 'hold' her smile in her fist. She must then 'throw' her smile to another player in the circle. This player should then 'catch' the smile and put it on her own face. She must then take off her smile and throw it to someone else, as before.

The only rule of this game is that only one player is allowed to smile at any one time. If any of the other players start to grin before they are thrown a smile, they are disqualified and must leave the circle. This game is a lot harder than it looks!

WINNING SMILES

To make the game extra funny, pull a really silly grin whenever it is your turn to be the Smiler. Open your eyes as wide as you can and open your lips to reveal all of your teeth. Or try smiling with your lips clamped shut and only smiling with your cheeks. Experiment with different smiles to see which one gets the most laughs.

HOW TO FORGIVE YOUR FRIEND

You and your friend have fallen out in a big way. She has really hurt your feelings, and even though she has apologized, there is no way that you will ever be able to make up ... or is there? Discover how you can rescue your friendship before it's too late.

TAKE A LOOK AT THE BIG PICTURE

Step back from the situation and take some time to think about what your friend has done to upset you. Try to think about the 'big picture' of your friendship. This means that instead of worrying and getting angry about this hurtful event, look back at all the time you have spent together and consider your friendship as it really is.

Think about why you are friends in the first place – for example, you may have been friends since you were very little, or perhaps you have both been great friends since you moved to a new school. Think of all the good times you have shared together and ask yourself, 'Is this argument worth throwing away our friendship?' The answer is nearly always, 'No.'

BE HONEST WITH YOURSELF

When you know someone better than anyone else does, it means you both know how to hurt each other more than anyone else does. When you are feeling angry about something your friend has said or done, ask yourself if you have ever done anything similar in the past – either to her or to anyone else. It can be really difficult to be this honest with yourself when your feelings have been hurt. But if you are able to admit that you have done some hurtful things in the past, you will find it much easier to forgive your friend.

CLEAR THE AIR

When your friend says she is sorry, let her know exactly why her words or actions hurt you. This way she knows what she is saying sorry for and has a chance to explain herself. Listen to her – then hug and make up.

FORGIVE AND FORGET

There is no point in forgiving your friend if you are going to remind her of what she did all of the time. If she has apologized and you have accepted it, try to leave it at that. If you keep on bringing up her mistake, she may get tired of hearing about how much she hurt you and decide to be friends with someone else.

True-friend tip. Being a good friend is a decision that you have to make every day. Sometimes this decision is easy, but when you have been hurt, it is much harder. Remember that if both of you still want to be friends, nothing can get in your way.

DARING DEEDS FOR BEST FRIENDS TO DO

Picture the scene: it's a Sunday afternoon, it's raining outside, there's nothing on TV, and you've even rearranged your bedroom out of boredom. Well, be bored no longer. Grab a friend and play a game of dares, and your afternoon will turn into a side-splitting adventure!

DARING RULES

The rules of daring are very simple. Take it in turns to set each other tricky tasks to complete. You are allowed two 'passes' each. These allow you to get out of doing any dare you don't like – use them very carefully.

DARING DEEDS

Here are ten dares to get you started, but think of some of your own.

Dare one. Put all your clothes on backwards and wear them out to the shop.

Dare two. Eat a mouthful of a weird combination of food – what about smelly cheese and banana, or cereal with orange juice on, or cold baked beans with jelly? Yuck!

Dare three. Pick up a spider or other insect, and hold it (gently!) enclosed in your palm for a full minute.

Dare four. Stand outside the front of your house and sing a really soppy love song at the top of your voice.

Dare five. Run up to the nearest boy and quickly kiss him on the cheek before he knows what hit him.

Dare six. Get your friend to write your name on your forehead in face paint then walk around the block with it on.

Dare seven. Try to drink a glass of water while standing on your head.

Dare eight. Put your dinner plate on the floor and eat from it like a dog.

Dare nine. Ignore anyone who speaks to you for the next 15 minutes, including your parents.

Dare ten. Go outside and pour an ice-cold cup of water over your head.

True-friend tip. Remember, games are supposed to be fun. Keep things friendly and make sure everyone knows that they don't have to do anything they really don't want to do.

HOW TO MAKE NEW FRIENDS

Whether you have just moved to a new town or just find it tricky to find fun friends to hang out with, follow these tips and you will soon find it easy to get chatting. You might even bag yourself a new best bud.

NEIGHBOURHOOD WATCH

Maybe you've seen some other kids playing near your house but have no idea how to start up a conversation? Ask an adult if they would mind you going outside near where they are hanging out and doing an activity that you can do alone that might get their attention – for example, roller-skating or cycling. If they seem interested in what you are doing, why not offer them a go on your skates or bike? If you smile and act friendly, you are sure to get chatting in no time.

GET INTERESTING

Having lots of interests outside of school hours is a fun way of finding and making new friends. Clubs and societies are great because you will often be put into groups with people and be made to work together. Whatever your interests, you are sure to find a group that reflects them, from basketball to drama to music – or ask your parents if you could join your local youth club or Girl Guides unit.

BE APPROACHABLE

If you make yourself look friendly, people will be more likely to want to strike up a conversation with you. Here's how this can be done.

DON'T look at the floor or your shoes. You won't find any new friends there!

DO smile and make eye-contact with people.

DO say, 'Hi.' It sounds obvious but a simple greeting can be enough to get the conversation rolling.

DON'T fold your arms. This makes you look 'closed off' and grumpy to others.

DO stand up straight, with your hands in your pockets or by your sides. This will make you look relaxed, confident and ready for some fun.

DON'T despair. You may not meet them right away, but your new friends are out there and can't wait to get to know you.

HOW TO WRITE A LETTER TO YOUR PEN FRIEND

You don't have to live in the same town or even country as someone to become friends. With a pen friend, you can get to know someone really well just by writing to them. Today, most people communicate by phone and email, but it's so exciting to receive an envelope in the post, addressed to you.

FIND A FRIEND

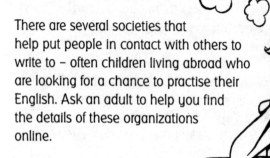

Ask a teacher at school if it is possible for her to contact another school somewhere else in the country to see if any of the pupils there would like to start writing to your class. If you are a Girl Guide, why not ask your unit leader to find another unit for you to write to?

There are several societies that help put people in contact with others to write to – often children living abroad who are looking for a chance to practise their English. Ask an adult to help you find the details of these organizations online.

PUT PEN TO PAPER

Now you have your pen friend, what do you write? Staring at a blank sheet of writing paper can be a bit daunting, so follow these top tips to achieve pen-pal perfection.

To begin. Take a sheet of writing paper and write your name and address in the top right-hand corner. Write today's date underneath. On the left-hand side of your paper write, 'Dear *your pen friend's name*' and follow this with a comma.

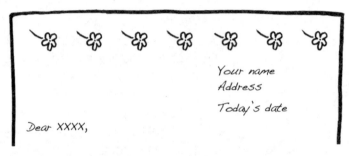

Your name
Address
Today's date

Dear XXXX,

Paragraph one. If your pen friend has written to you already, thank them for the letter. Introduce yourself. Tell her your name and your age and where you go to school. You might want to tell her about your family and whether you have any brothers or sisters. End the paragraph with a question – for example, 'Do you have any brothers or sisters?'

Paragraph two. Tell your pen friend something interesting that you have done recently – for example, 'On Saturday I had some friends over for a sleepover. We had a midnight feast, and it was great fun! What do you like to do at the weekend?'

Paragraph three. Tell your pen friend a secret or something really cool about your life – for example, 'My best friends are called Sara and Annabel – we call ourselves "The Glam Stars" and are starting our own band. Who are your best friends?'

Paragraph four. The last paragraph should be a conclusion. Write about how much you are looking forward to hearing back from her, and ask anything else you would like to know about her life.

Saying goodbye. As this is an informal letter, you can sign off with 'Best wishes' followed by a comma, then sign your name.

SEND THE LETTER

Before you fold your letter and seal it in an envelope, check that you have written your address properly and make any corrections. Then pop your letter into the envelope.

Write your pen pal's name and address on the front of your envelope and stick a stamp in the top right-hand corner. Now post off your scribblings. Hopefully, in a few days or weeks, you will be receiving a letter filled with exciting news.

Daisy Day
15 Happy Avenue
Middletown
Friendshipshire
FR8 5NY

True-friend tip. If you are writing to somebody who lives in a foreign country, you will need to go to your nearest post office and ask how many stamps you need to put on your letter, as it will cost more to send it overseas.

THREE INSTANT BOREDOM-BUSTERS FOR YOU AND YOUR FRIENDS

Even the most fun friends can have dull days every now and again. Keep monotonous moments at bay with these quick and easy boredom-busters.

THE ACCENT TRICK

It's good to play the 'Accent Trick' in a public place where you will have to speak to lots of other people – for example: in cafés, on buses or at sports centres. Choose a foreign accent that you and your friends are quite confident using. American or Australian accents are good choices, as we are used to hearing the accents in films and on TV. Before you start, practise your accent to make sure it sounds realistic. Then the idea is to pass yourselves off as a person of a different nationality in public. Make sure you keep a straight face at all times or the game will be up. Throw in some realistic-sounding detail – for example, if you are in a library, whisper to your friend, 'Back home in the States, the libraries only let you take out one book at a time ...' See how long you can keep it up!

BACKSEAT BINGO

'Backseat Bingo' is a great way of having fun when you are on a long car journey or on the coach on a school trip. Before you leave, make your bingo cards as shown opposite – one for each friend. Each player needs one of the cards and a pen. When you spot one of the items on your card, you should call out that you have seen it. Once everyone has also seen it, you can cross it off your card. The first person to cross off all of the things on their card shouts, 'Bingo!' and they are the winner.

Teacher/parent tells us to 'Ssssshhhh!'	A roundabout.	A white van overtakes us on the road.	Someone's mobile phone rings.
A horse in a field.	An advert on the radio.	A café by the roadside.	A petrol station.

THUMB WAR

'Thumb war' is a two-player game. Stick out your right hands as if you are about to shake hands. Curl your fingers around your friend's fingers and stick your thumbs up in the air. To begin the game, both chant: 'One, two, three, four, I declare a thumb war. Five, six, seven, eight – try to keep your thumb straight!' The aim of the game is to pin your friend's thumb underneath your own without unlinking your fingers from hers. Once you have your opponent's thumb held down underneath yours, you say: 'One, two, three, four, I have won the thumb war!' You win if you manage to hold her thumb down for the time it takes you to say the rhyme. If they escape, the game's still on!

HOW TO START A GIRL BAND

If you love music, starting a band with your friends can be serious fun! Practising together and making up songs is a real buzz, and can lead to playing performances in public, and entering competitions. You might even set off on the road to superstardom. Here's how to get started.

WHAT TO PLAY?

The first thing to think about is what kind of a girl band you want to be. Do you imagine yourself and your friends rocking out on stage with guitars and drums? Are you more of a group of pop princesses with a killer sense of style?

ROCK YOUR SOCKS OFF

If you decide on a rock-chick image for your band, you'll probably want to play your own instruments. Buying your own can get very expensive – check with your teacher if it is possible for you all to join a music club at school where you can use the instruments.

In the meantime, you need to work on your most important instruments – your voices. Practise singing 'a cappella' as much as you can, which means singing together or on your own without any instruments. Singing a cappella will help you to get your voices working together and doesn't cost a penny. Most talent shows ask you to audition a cappella in the first rounds, so get used to it now so that you can wow the judges when the time comes.

DANCING QUEENS

If you want your band to belt out some chart-topping pop hits, then playing musical instruments isn't as important as a series of slick dance moves and some serious singing. Watch lots of music videos for inspiration, and decide whether your band will have one lead singer and some brilliant backing singers, or whether you will all take turns at singing solo.

Try to link your dance moves to the feeling of your song. If it's a fast, exciting song, you could try hip-hop style moves with lots of energy. If it's a love song, you could all stand in a line and perform small movements, such as clicking the fingers of one hand in time to the rhythm.

Try to imagine performing in front of a big crowd, even when you're just practising in your bedroom, and incorporate some moves that will get the audience bopping along, such as waving your arms above your head or clapping your hands in time to the beat and encouraging them to do the same.

GO YOUR OWN WAY

The most important thing for any girl group is a sense of individuality. Whether you decide to sing songs that you have written yourselves, or to belt out your version of a current smash hit, it's really important to add your own style and personality to your songs. Give it that star quality that will make people fall in love with your band.

Think about the different personalities of the members of your band, and try to show them off in the way that each of you dress, and the signature moves that each of you has. For example, if one of your friends is very girly and sweet, her 'band uniform' could include a lot of pink, and her signature move could be blowing the audience kisses.

True-friend tip. Get together with your band mates regularly to brainstorm great new song and dance ideas, and to make sure that everyone is happy with their place in the band.

HOW TO STAY FRIENDS FOR LIFE

Okay, so you are great friends now, but what about in the future? Make sure that you stay best buddies for life by following these top tips.

FOREVER FRIENDS

Promise to be there. Pick a place that is special to you and your friend and promise to meet there at 5 pm on August 1st every five years, without fail!

Accept the fact that you will both change. As you grow older, you and your friend will both change and may become quite different from each other. If you accept this change, it can actually make your friendship stronger and more interesting, rather than destroying it.

Be birthday buddies. Always remember each other's birthdays. Buy a special 'Birthday Book' to write the dates in, and then you'll have no excuse for forgetting!

Don't let boys come between you. Remember that crushes on boys come and go, while friends are always there.

Remember that newer doesn't mean better. There is an old saying, 'Make new friends, but don't forget the old, for one is silver and the other, gold.' Always try to remember this.

Keep smiling. When life gets serious, keep making each other laugh!

Distance doesn't mean doom. If one of you has to move away, see if it is possible to visit them on holiday.

Put pen to paper. Keep in contact by writing and sending each other photos, even if you move thousands of miles away. You can do this by letter and on the internet. There is no excuse for letting things slide.

True-friend tip. Try to forgive your friend if she sometimes forgets about you. As you get older, and when you have families of your own, life can get busy and friends can sometimes get temporarily forgotten about. As long as you make the effort to stay in contact, your friendship will survive.

HOW TO MAKE EVERLASTING FRIENDSHIP CAKE

Cake can always be enjoyed with friends, but this cake is different. This is a cake that grows with your friendship and can be passed around for years to come. Like friendships, it takes a little effort to keep going, but the outcome is definitely worth it.

You will need:

Day one:

- 100 g plain flour • 225 ml water
  - $\frac{1}{2}$ sachet fast-acting yeast

Day two and Day seven:

- 100 g plain flour • 225 ml water
  - 200 g caster sugar

Day twelve:

- 1 egg, beaten • 125 g plain flour
- $\frac{3}{4}$ teaspoon sodium bicarbonate
  - 100 ml vegetable oil
- 1 teaspoon baking powder • $\frac{1}{2}$ teaspoon salt
  - 1 teaspoon vanilla extract
  - 5 very ripe bananas, mashed

DAY ONE

1. Pour the flour into a small bowl and add the yeast. Stir together well, then add the water. Cover the bowl loosely with plastic wrap and put to one side (not in the fridge) for 24 hours. This is called your 'starter mix'.

DAY TWO

2. Remove the plastic wrap from the bowl and add the flour, water and caster sugar from the Day two ingredients on the previous page. Stir this together well until all the flour is mixed in. Cover the bowl with plastic wrap and then pop it in the fridge.

EVERY DAY AFTER DAY TWO FOR FIVE DAYS

3. Take the bowl out of the fridge, remove the plastic wrap and give the starter mix a good stir. Replace the plastic wrap and pop it back in the fridge.

DAY SEVEN

4. Repeat steps **2** and **3**.

DAY TWELVE

5. Ask an adult to preheat the oven to Gas Mark 4/180°C.

6. Grease a 23 x 13 cm loaf tin by dipping a piece of kitchen paper into a little butter and wiping the butter all over the inside of the tin until it is covered with grease.

7. Take your starter mix out of the fridge and give it a good stir. Measure out 300 ml, using a measuring jug, and pour this into a large mixing bowl. Put the rest of your starter mix back into the fridge.

8. Add the rest of the ingredients and stir together well with a wooden spoon, until it is all combined and there are no lumps of flour. Don't worry about lumps of banana, they will just make it super-tasty.

9. Pour the mixture into the greased loaf tin and ask an adult to put it into the oven for 35 minutes.

10. Ask an adult to remove the cake from the oven and put it to one side to cool. You can now eat your friendship cake for afternoon tea.

11. Remove the rest of your starter mix from the fridge and divide it into three equally sized portions. Keep one portion for yourself but pour the other two into two, clean glass jars/plastic containers with lids.

12. Give the jars to friends and tell them to follow steps **2** to **11**. Giving them a ready-made starter mix means they can skip step **1** altogether. Soon they will be able to make their own fabulous friendship cake and pass on some starter mix to other friends.

13. Follow steps **2** to **11** with your own left-over starter mix and you will soon have yet another yummy cake and more starter mix to pass on.

True-friend tip. Why not experiment with different flavours? Replace the mashed banana with chopped apple and raisins or even chocolate chips and nuts. Look after your starter mix and it will last you for years.

HOW TO MAKE FRIENDS WITH YOUR PARENTS

Think about it: only your very best friend knows you better than your parents do. Parents can teach you loads of cool new stuff, and you might find that they give you lots more freedom once you understand each other better. Follow these handy hints to make your folks your friends.

PERFECT PARENT POINTERS

Ask them to teach you something. All grown-ups love to feel that they are experts on something. Here's your chance to learn some cool new skills from your parents, and maybe get a bit closer.

Tell them about your day. Answering questions about your day when you just want to relax can be a real drag. To avoid this, tell your parents a couple of things without being asked, and you'll be free to get on with your evening much sooner. It doesn't have to be anything special – for example, tell them about a new game you played at break time, or how much you like your new class project.

Find out what makes them tick. After all, they have got their own likes, dislikes and hobbies, just like you. Find out what your dad's favourite music is. You may just discover some cool retro bands that you love as much as he does. If you spend time working out what they love, you'll learn more about them and you'll get on with them much better.

HOW TO HOLD A SWAP SHOP

When your pocket money doesn't quite stretch to a shopping spree, a swap shop is a great way to bag yourself some goodies for free. You'll have fun, too. Remember, one person's trash is another's treasure. Here's how.

THREE TO FOUR WEEKS BEFORE

Ask your parents' permission first, then send out invitations to your friends as follows:

You are invited to:

Maxine's Swap Shop!

Date: 11th November
Place: Maxine's House
Time: 11am

Please bring a bag or box full of your
unwanted clothes, books, CDs and anything
else you want to swap.

TWO WEEKS BEFORE

Start assembling your own collection of items to swap. Anything broken is probably not going to be very popular, but clothes you have gone off or grown out of might be perfect for one of your friends. Everyone is a different size and shape and has different tastes, so your cast-offs could be their dream outfits! You could also ask any older siblings or friends if they have anything they'd like to donate – they may have outgrown some very cool bits and pieces.

THE DAY BEFORE

Make sure you have a clear space in the house for holding the swap shop. Buy or make any snacks you want to serve for the hungry swappers (see page 34 for ideas).

ON THE DAY

Lay out your own items for swapping on the floor or on a table. When your friends arrive they can lay out their items, too. Then the swap shop is open!

You can either go round the group, asking people to introduce their items and anyone who wants them just shouts out. Alternatively, your swap shop can be like a free jumble sale where everyone wanders about and picks what they fancy. You can use a downstairs loo or behind a door as a dressing room if people are bashful about trying clothes on in front of each other.

THE RULES OF THE SWAP

• Only one bagful of stuff to be taken home per person – don't get greedy.

• No secretly reserving stuff before the swap has officially begun.

• Be kind about people's cast-offs – they might not be to your taste but everyone is different!

• If two people want the same item, the original owner gives it to the person who offers them something they want to swap with.

True-friend tip. Try on everything you have your eye on – there's no point ending up with loads more clothes that don't fit when you've just got rid of a batch.

SWAP UNTIL YOU DROP

Hooray! You should now have at least one whole 'new' outfit to wear plus lots more goodies that are 'new' to you. There may be items left over which no one has taken. If so, donate them to your local charity shop.

ALSO AVAILABLE ...

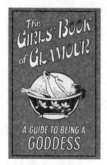

The Girls' Book Of Glamour:
A Guide To Being
A Goddess

ISBN: 978-1-906082-13-0

The Fabulous Girls' Book:
Discover The Secret
Of Being Fabulous

ISBN: 978-1-906082-52-9

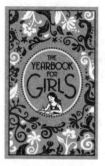

The Girls' Book Of Secrets:
Shhh ... Don't Tell!

ISBN: 978-1-906082-38-3

The Yearbook
For Girls

ISBN: 978-1-906082-82-6

The Girls' Book 1:
How To Be The Best
At Everything

The Girls' Book 2:
How To Be The Best
At Everything Again

The Girls' Book 3:
Even More Ways To Be
The Best At Everything

ISBN: 978-1-905158-79-9 ISBN: 978-1-906082-32-1 ISBN: 978-1-906082-76-5